What
was it like
Before
Television?

Rosie Hankin

Illustrated by
Diana Bowles

Evans

We used the clothes from
her dressing-up box.

We often used to make up plays when I
was young. In those days there was no
television to watch.

5

It must have been boring without television.

Children had lots to do before television was invented. Look at all the games in my old toy cupboard.

Tell us about the games you played when you were a child.

7

Before television was invented people
played board games and card games.

What is this game?

8

9

My sisters made a stamp collection and
a coin collection when they were little.

*Look, these stamps are beautiful!
They came from India.*

They used steam to get the stamps
off postcards and envelopes.
My father always helped them.

12

I loved collecting pretty pictures and postcards to stick into my scrap-book. My mother made glue for me out of flour and water.

My mother taught me to sew. I learned to do crochet and embroidery, too.

14

I wish I could crochet.

15

On fine evenings we used to play outside.
Sometimes we made our own toys.

We loved making paper kites like these to fly on windy days.

I'm going to fly my kite outside when it's ready.

The roads were safer when I was little
because there were fewer cars.
We used to play in the street with
our friends.

*Let's play hopscotch
in the garden, now.*

My parents took us to the cinema
once a week. We always saw two
films and a newsreel.

Now we can watch the news on television at home.

21

My parents sometimes took us to
the music hall for a special treat.
We joined in all the songs and
laughed at the comedian.

I tried to remember the songs
so that I could sing them
when we got
home.

When I was young I played the piano
and my brother played the violin.
We often played duets together.

My mother played the piano, too.
Sometimes she would play and
sing to us.

24

25

We sometimes listened to the
news on the wireless.
There were special
programmes for
children, too.

My father always read us a story
before we went to sleep.

We did have fun when I was little. We couldn't watch television but there were plenty of other things to do.

29

The children on this page are very busy. Do you know what they are all doing? The answers are at the bottom of the page, but don't peep until you have tried yourself.

1.

2.

4.

3.

Answers: 1. Listening to the wireless 2. Making a scrap-book 3. Collecting stamps 4. Playing draughts 5. Playing the violin